island

candy neubert

the colophon press

published by The Colophon Press
with support of Arts Council England

© candy neubert
ISBN 978-0-9566469-0-3

All rights reserved. No part of this
publication may be reproduced, stored
in a retrieval system, or transmitted
in any form, electronic, photo copying
or otherwise, without prior permission

cover The Blue Pool
by Augustus John

cover design by Louis

info@thecolophonpress.co.uk

typeset and printing by
Kingfisher Print & Design

contents

privacy	5
navigating	6
inlet	7
the harbour	8
eyes shut	12
granite	13
shoal	14
canaries	15
channel	16
here are pebbles	17
picnic	18
salt	20
afternoon	21
tide (i)	22
tide (ii)	24
tide (iii)	26
warm sea	28
ashes	29
rocquaine	30
stone	31
island	32

privacy

I have come home.
This room is my room
and the wind, restless outside,
driving the sea hard against the shore,
is mine,
and the salt smell
driving into my nose, mine,
and the bus which so slowly passed
hedges and field, the tractor turning left,
is mine, and when the driver says
do you want to get out here
I do
and the man in reception
is handing me the key.

navigating

Let's board a boat, shall we,
and then forget the harbour.
We'll look back at nothing, and then wonder,
is it the wind or a current, taking us so fast?
Let's wait for dark, and have no oars,
or rudder even, and a bare mast.

inlet

There's only one coastline to trace again;
that is what happens when you dream islands.
Mostly it's high tide, the water milk green
right over the road, deep on the slipways,
sunlight moving slow across the sea wall
between bits of weed. Turning the corner
the air is sharp, the horizon purple.
This isn't happiness you remember,
but longing; how the cold of that water
takes the skin, how love is an obsession,
they say. They can use any word they like.
See those small white cottages – one of them
is yours; float from one inlet to the next
over and over, trying all the doors.

the harbour

I said time
between island and island
was time timeless
but it seems you did not see.
Important I explain
you understand
about the drops of land
we come across.

At the beginning is the harbour
with the many steps;
a telephone at night,
the trunks of trees and crates
along the quay. The tide laps up
and falls for miles, downward,
when it falls. Lean out between the houses,
see how far, and what strange green from
centuries before.

That is the harbour
with the soundless ships. Below
the concrete and the wood are always wet,
the dripping smell of world
and weed left hanging by the fuse
of pillars with the sea.

So many people leave this way.
Some in a hurry, though the moves of men
create no echoes here. Sometimes
a Chinese water boat will bear
a row of silent heads;
sometimes I sit across the walls
with legs on either side
and high winds pick me off.
I have been watching at the harbour
since a child, and since before that time.
He often comes this way.

There is a boat that leaves each day
though years may come between
the rising of one gangplank and the next,
the metal link through link around a wheel.

I nearly took the boat the day
it sank chaotic in the harbour mouth.
I ran to see it pull away
with sucking motion from the dock
and heave before the open sea,
before the eyes
of all the sudden crowd along the rail.

Of many hands at work to pull
the bodies from the water, I was one.
Not grieving for the dead, nor glad for life,
we worked in rhythm and the rain;

I heard them say too bad for you,
they said that you were there,
they brought you streaming up from stone
and laid you on the pier.

The home town rises up,
exultant in the moment crossed
from dream to death.
The wet cold sand, salt smell, the level sea,
the path of sun in triangles
that yield and pull, mid-ocean.

This is the harbour of the heaving line
slap slapping in the smell of oil,
the lifting ships, the men leap
one to one, a little drunk;
the tiny fish in clouds under the dock.
Another port to pass.
There goes the telephone,
here comes the music, up the mast and cables
snapping in the wind.

This is the harbour,
there the steps,
this is the way,
there is the helping hand.

Important you should know
just how it was to leave
and turn inland,
as those preparing for the sea
survive the land.

Important you should know
just how it is to leave the harbour,
being sure there is a cause,
that something matters beyond any doubt.

eyes shut

Each house has its own tiny front garden
and a name like Bel Air or San Souci.
She reads them to me, pushing the pushchair
while I find magic, down in a crevice,
learning to feel for it with my fingers,
keeping myself still, keeping my eyes shut.
There are high walls I walk along the top
and pointy ones I can't, running my hands
over their surface between the railings,
racing ahead to where the pavement ends
and then she calls out to me sharply, stop.

We must go on. I leave her, I grow up,
I'm hurrying in the same direction
back to the burrow like a crazed rabbit.
I took off with the map unravelling
in my head, one lane after another,
one more bloody field, one more damn valley,
crossing the entire length of the island
with my lungs on fire to find out how,
keeping myself still, keeping my eyes shut,
I could have something so incredible
it would save me for the rest of my life.

granite

She stands at the sea wall, its stone
holding the sun, the early morning cold,
and yesterday's sun, deepest of all.
The wind is at her legs; she pulls the towel
– a salt smell in its fibre,
from the stone, and from the sand.
The sea spreads out, cupped far away
in the open palm of the land.

Down there, alone, the high tide barely turned
and swilling at the wall, the boy stands,
hugging his surfboard.

He looks back over his shoulder,
making sure she watches him in this wide sea
to pin him to the surface, to exist. And she
is him, not only leaning on the wall
but down there too, cold water at her waist.
And time between
the standing at the wall and in the sea
becomes one thing which curves,
its two ends meeting, easily.

shoal

It was years ago I swam in the west
when the sun went down and waves
lifted a shoal of fish, the light behind them
catching each one gold.

So long ago you can't remember
if you swam with me or it was someone else
or I was just there by myself
and told you later. I was definitely

there and waves came up
over and over smooth and high
and broke on me and came again
with fish in, and behind them, light.

canaries

In the Plaza de Asturias at noon a woman
runs up the steps to be photographed, smiling,
and a thin girl sits on the next bench
with a man who lays his head in her lap,
one arm around her back at the same time.
A little later she protests: señor! and takes off
between the trees, looking back once,
but the man lies on the seat, finished with her.
Another nearby reads Kahlil Gibran; the waiter
with the long black trouser legs walks round and round,
two men with cigarettes stroll by with prams
and there are girls, and birds, which are canaries.
On the flagstones at my feet, spit.

The girl comes back, walking slowly, kicking dust,
dipping her fingers in the fountain
and flicking them over the man, but she's already
fixed and written and the spit dry,
the man not only finished with her by now
– he's fast asleep with his hat over his face,
and even though the canaries are still singing
she can sit as long as she likes over there,
gazing at the man who has something she wants,
like the other end of a bad quarrel perhaps,
or money; however long she sits it's clearly
too late, spreading her hands in annoyance
as if the world is watching, which I am.

channel

sat on the sea wall as if all the world
was everywhere a sea wall and the sand
always spread out at my feet into light
and rock and rock pools and the bright channels
unroll their way down to a falling tide
as if always the heat of this long day
lay in the stone under my thighs as if
my skin would carry the crisp burn of salt
my shin and ankle bone be rough with it
my body ready to run into it
tomorrow or later or again now
as if thirst would anywhere only be
broken by this pushing out of my depth
out of my self out into open sea

here are pebbles

She tries to get nearer; she moves along
the rows in the fine dust of the greenhouse,
slowly watering the base of each plant.
Back in the kitchen an hour before,
picnic things into a basket, a fold
of towels, the hour which made this hour
following to the path's end and the rail
where she leans, waiting. At the same moment
here are pebbles, cool from the falling tide,
slow back somersaults in the green water
– all of it here, gradually unpacking,
sandwiches in their foil, a paper bag
of tomatoes. Sand. Light. None of it gone,
none of it lost, none of it even past.

picnic

there was a paler stone
which fit her back

she spread her wrap
and sat on it

I hung my costume
where one jutted out

he hung his on a groyne
with a rock on top

I didn't know
they didn't say

you will come back
one day to this

will turn exactly
to this place

sure as a seabird
to the cliff

think how we always
went in first

emerging salty
one by one

happy to wait
for who came last

before we opened up
the basket

salt

all day long
I've been going to the beach
which is amazing
when you think
how far this is
from the sea

afternoon

On the way from one rockpool to another,
imagine someone calls.
Right in the middle of a bright afternoon,
with the sky grey in a far corner
                       and the sea beckoning,
your own name called.

You can't disobey but you can be difficult.
You can drag all the way over the stones
                       and across the sand,
up the steps, into the car park,
all through the unlocking of the door
                       and the back seat.
Time to leave.

Down the corridor we go. There's a hand
                       under your arm
and you're heading somewhere.
Come along, says the voice, but you drag
                       all the way.
Who cares about the day finishing; who knows
about a bright afternoon left in the middle,
and the sea beckoning, and your own name?

tide (i)

my love it is after
we close on the land
and I reckon the distance
between islands

wondering how deep
wondering how far
and if the wind will rise

it is after
I am already waiting
that I hear you call

you are there
on the turn of the stairs
thinking hard

I stand in front of you
breathing

you show me the place
where it cannot be helped

a simple embrace
writes itself
on your chest

how dark it is love
how you move your long hands

my heart has grown still
in my whole body
yes

tide (ii)

our cabin is damp and salt my love
I sink myself
into this sea
over these rocks

the ship comes white
between the islands
and you lean across the rail
happy

still you walk
along the wind-flat north
lifting the sheets
or is it me
begging you in

passing the chair
where you write
in a lamp-lit pool
you beautiful
lighting the back of my neck

turning the handle
quietly
shut

down wooden steps
down the wet grass

tumbling the dark my love
where you might see

tide (iii)

my love
up here among the ropes
it is a long way down

how do they sleep like this
slung in the mooring lines

it is a long way down
my heart
I see you
on the busy pier

the water shines
under the lamps

cold air comes up from it
softly

I see you pause
to check your scarf
and how you look
in a warehouse window

watch beloved
watch me turn

the bow drifts in
against the wall

before she swings
watch me beloved
stand
and in that second
step

warm sea

Put the old people into the warm sea.
Lift them gently up and put them in.

Their limbs love green water.
Their feet enjoy the sand.

Old women forget the brown stains on their hands.
They are happy as girls.

Old men find muscle on their bones,
enough to float.

It is better than cake.
It is better than grandchildren.

But, old people don't travel well,
so put them near the warm sea while they're young.

ashes

I made you promise
to put my dead body in a boat
and set it alight

you were good with petrol and wood
you could lift any old dinghy
your hands were made for the job

I ran round to your house
with my eyes all mad
and made you promise

I said promise you won't let me
get stuck on this island not even my ashes
I won't be able to breathe

you looked up from your varnishing
and sighed and said yeah yeah

rocquaine

I go back there, you see, or the houses
come to me; I can't say how often,
there is no often,
there's salt and horizon
and the cottages lie down behind
their little white walls.
We melt and turn the walls and sometimes
pull out long passages.

I'm married, you see.
It doesn't matter if there are no flowers
– that's not my way, but I am still
his wife, and we drive up in his car
and stop out there
in the dark by the sea wall.
It's my place or his and he won't help,
that's not his way, and we sit

in silence, you see, with the waves
falling on our right, and the Hanois
lights up spray on the windscreen
every few minutes.
I push my face into his coat
and he lets me, or he pulls away
if it's his house,
and I stand by the window, drowned.

stone

and I will tell nobody
I am come back to you
no one who saw me
walk abroad
would guess that I was true

no man think how particular
I choose my little lane
the warmth of it
telling my feet
that they are here again

the quiet hedges lead me
where I can see your home
so nearly buried
in the dark
so thick the layers
where I slip
through such resistant stone

island

Crouched on the floor, the sand under his knees,
this is the last night on the island.
No gulls call, no late cars on the road.
The tamarisk thrashes out there.

He's full of it,
        full of his boyhood in the lanes.
He walks the cliff, a shell picked clean.

When he come back, he is a ghost.

—

The children sleep.
The house is more than quiet.
Their breathing fills the room and every space
        between the walls
and all the stone and all the mortar porous with it,
        in and out.

—

The bleat of pigeons.

He's not reading: he allows something
which here in England is called doing nothing.

Cool of summer at his feet.

tick tick tick tick

A wave against a wall
        acknowledged by a person far inland.

The hour more full than any out there,
opening his mouth.

—

He runs all the way down the pavement
        towards the cemetery
and there is his mother,
walking freely without pain,
pushing the pram.

He loves the graveyard with its rising hill,
        hiding the bodies.
Up this path and down that, alive.

—

The island crosses, bends,
        and doubles back.
He walks without a moon, without his eyes.